Hadrian's Wall

Hadrian's Wall

Photographed by Theo Bergström

Bergström & Boyle Books, London

Produced and published by Bergström + Boyle Books Limited
22 Maddox Street, London W1R 9PG

Designed by John Hine

Photographs © Theo Bergström 1975
Text   © Sandy Boyle   1975

Made and printed in Great Britain by
Westerham Press Ltd, Westerham, Kent
Reproduction :—
Medway Reprographic Ltd, Tunbridge Wells.

Acknowledgement is made to Harold Hill and Son
for their permission to reproduce diagrams of
the Broad Wall, Narrow Wall, Turf Wall, Temple
of Antenociticus, Birdoswald Fort and cross
section of the Vallum earthworks from the
12th Edition of the Handbook to the Roman
Wall edited by Sir Ian Richmond

The diagrams of Chesters fort and bath house,
Housesteads fort are Crown Copyright reproduced
with the permission of the Controller of
Her Majesty's Stationery Office

The map is based on the Ordnance Survey map
'Hadrian's Wall' 1972. Crown Copyright reserved

ISBN Paper 0 903767 02 3
ISBN Boards 0 903767 03 1

The photographs in this book were taken on the line of Hadrian's Wall from Bowness-on-Solway in the west to Wallsend in the east.

For over two hundred and fifty years Roman soldiers guarded the wild northern frontier of their province of Britain, patrolling the high wall which crossed the country from sea to sea, and defending the barrier against the barbarians of southern Scotland.

Even today it is hard not to be impressed by the scale of the wall and its flanking earthworks, which were ordered by the Emperor Hadrian in A.D.122 and completed within ten years. In many places the remains can still be seen, relentlessly taking the best strategic line over moors and crags, and commanding magnificent views over the panoramic wastes to the north. The Cumbrian and Northumbrian countryside which Hadrian's Wall crosses is no less spectacular even where little trace of the Wall is left.

The pictures are followed by an illustrated map which will give you an idea of the visible remains, and what can be seen of interest at each site.

Northern Britain in Roman Times

The construction of the Wall was commissioned by the Roman Emperor Hadrian during his visit to the province of Britain in A.D. 122. He appointed a friend, Platorius Nepos, as governor to supervise the building of a wall eighty Roman miles long from the Tyne to the Solway, which would act as the northern frontier of the Roman Empire and keep the tribes of southern Scotland separate from those of northern England.

The Roman engineers designed a stone wall ten feet wide and fifteen feet high, taking every natural advantage of the lie of the land. **Milecastles** with barrack accommodation for about thirty men were constructed every Roman mile, and between each milecastle there were two **turrets**—possibly thirty feet high—used both for watching enemy movements to the north and signalling.

The first section of the Wall, from Newcastle to near Chesters, conformed to this plan, but for reasons of economy later stretches were built to a narrower gauge. The western part was first constructed in turf because of a shortage of local limestone, but quickly replaced in stone. A ditch ran the length of the Wall on the north side except where the steep ground made this unnecessary.

The original plan was to man this military frontier with a patrolling garrison. The fighting garrisons were stationed in the forts built some forty years earlier by Agricola along the **Stanegate**—a military road running from Carlisle to Corbridge—which is the earliest known frontier system in Britain. However the Britons proved more hostile than expected and during the building the plan had to be modified. Regular army units were then placed on the Wall itself in new forts like Housesteads and Chesters.

Later, a wide flatbottomed ditch, known as the **Vallum,** was built to the south side of the Wall in order to bar civilians from entry to the Wall area; and a military supply road—**the Military Way**—was constructed between the Vallum and the Wall.

During the latter part of Hadrian's reign the Wall was also extended from Newcastle to Wallsend, and shore defences were placed down the Cumberland coast to complete the frontier.

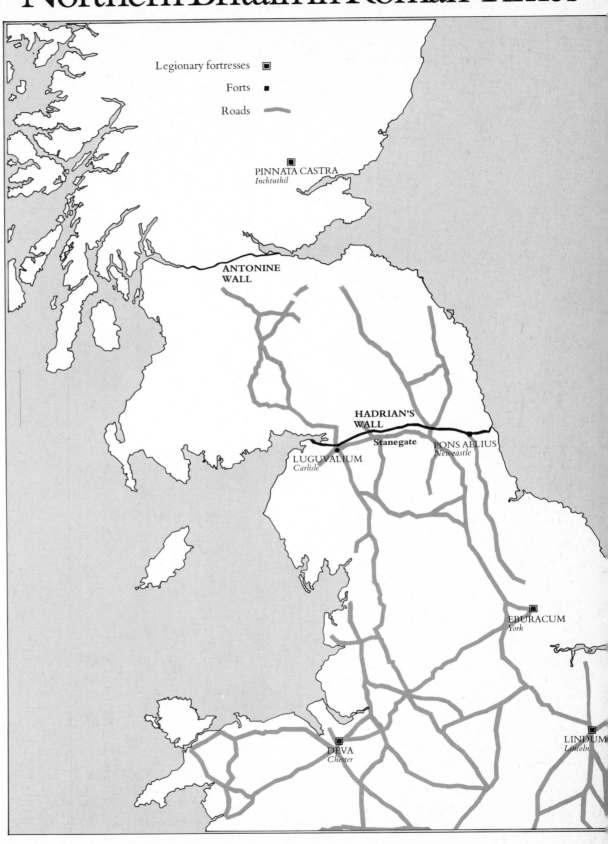

Legionary fortresses ■

Forts ■

Roads

PINNATA CASTRA
Inchtuthil

ANTONINE WALL

HADRIAN'S WALL

Stanegate

PONS AELIUS
Newcastle

LUGUVALIUM
Carlisle

EBURACUM
York

DEVA
Chester

LINDUM
Lincoln

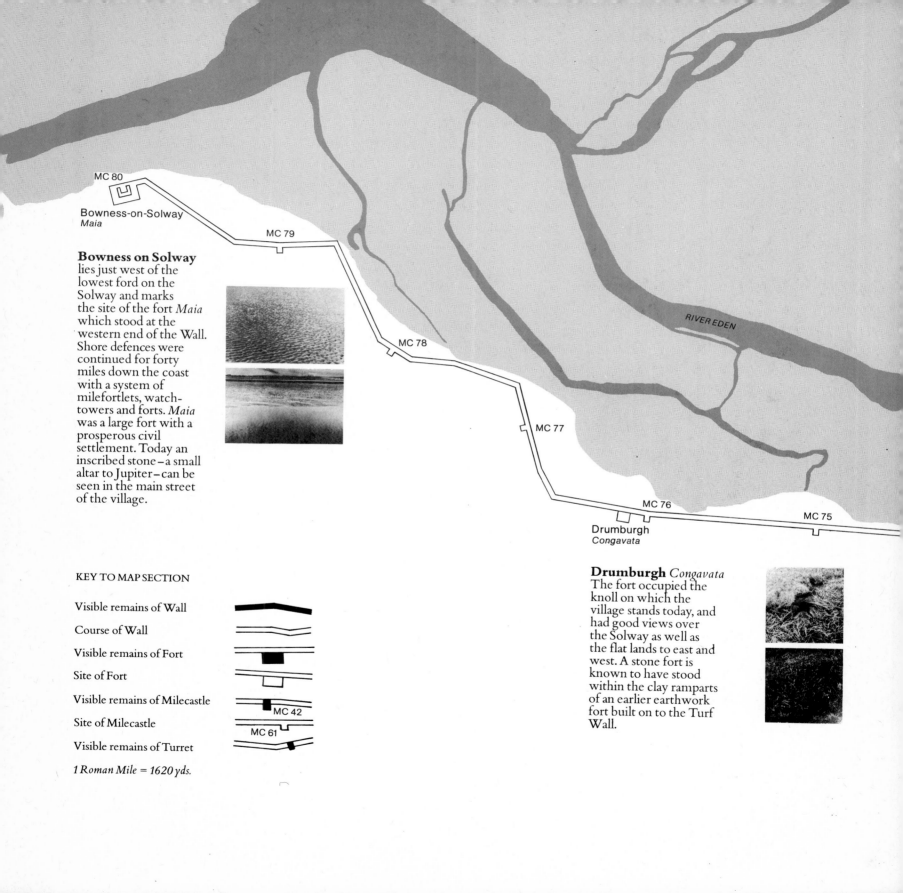

MC 80

Bowness-on-Solway
Maia

MC 79

MC 78

MC 77

MC 76

MC 75

Drumburgh
Congavata

RIVER EDEN

Bowness on Solway
lies just west of the
lowest ford on the
Solway and marks
the site of the fort *Maia*
which stood at the
western end of the Wall.
Shore defences were
continued for forty
miles down the coast
with a system of
milefortlets, watch-
towers and forts. *Maia*
was a large fort with a
prosperous civil
settlement. Today an
inscribed stone – a small
altar to Jupiter – can be
seen in the main street
of the village.

Drumburgh *Congavata*
The fort occupied the
knoll on which the
village stands today, and
had good views over
the Solway as well as
the flat lands to east and
west. A stone fort is
known to have stood
within the clay ramparts
of an earlier earthwork
fort built on to the Turf
Wall.

KEY TO MAP SECTION

Visible remains of Wall

Course of Wall

Visible remains of Fort

Site of Fort

Visible remains of Milecastle

MC 42

Site of Milecastle

MC 61

Visible remains of Turret

1 Roman Mile = 1620 yds.

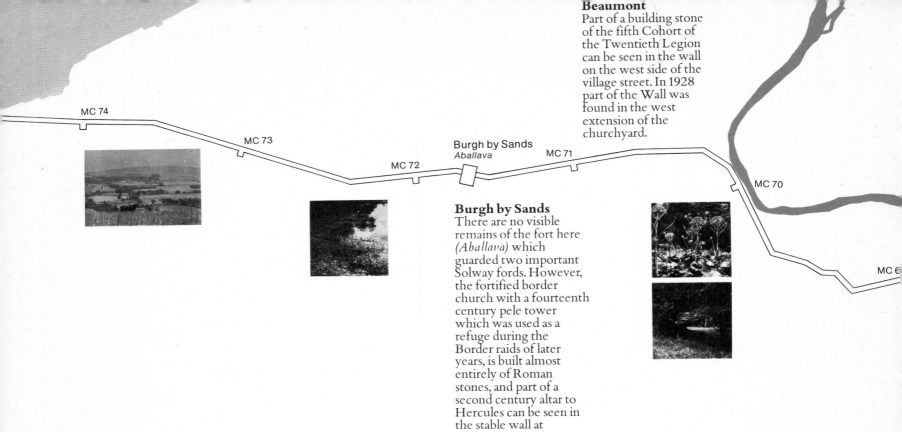

MC 74

MC 73

MC 72

Burgh by Sands
Aballava

MC 71

MC 70

MC 6

Beaumont
Part of a building stone of the fifth Cohort of the Twentieth Legion can be seen in the wall on the west side of the village street. In 1928 part of the Wall was found in the west extension of the churchyard.

Burgh by Sands
There are no visible remains of the fort here (*Aballava*) which guarded two important Solway fords. However, the fortified border church with a fourteenth century pele tower which was used as a refuge during the Border raids of later years, is built almost entirely of Roman stones, and part of a second century altar to Hercules can be seen in the stable wall at Cross Farm.

A building stone at Beaumont

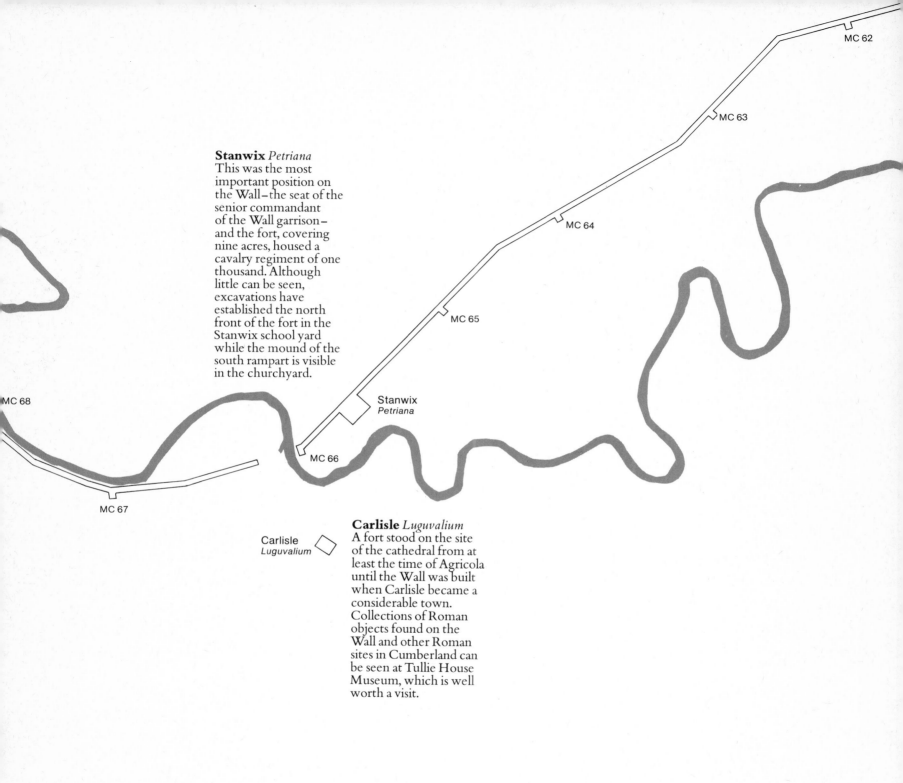

MC 62

MC 63

MC 64

Stanwix *Petriana*
This was the most
important position on
the Wall–the seat of the
senior commandant
of the Wall garrison–
and the fort, covering
nine acres, housed a
cavalry regiment of one
thousand. Although
little can be seen,
excavations have
established the north
front of the fort in the
Stanwix school yard
while the mound of the
south rampart is visible
in the churchyard.

MC 65

MC 68

Stanwix
Petriana

MC 66

MC 67

Carlisle
Luguvalium

Carlisle *Luguvalium*
A fort stood on the site
of the cathedral from at
least the time of Agricola
until the Wall was built
when Carlisle became a
considerable town.
Collections of Roman
objects found on the
Wall and other Roman
sites in Cumberland can
be seen at Tullie House
Museum, which is well
worth a visit.

Lanercost Priory

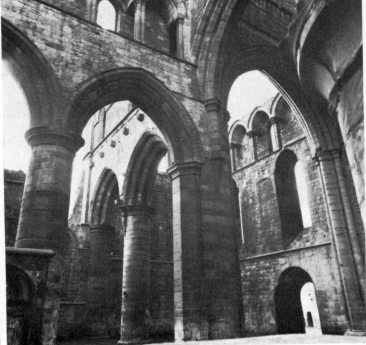

Lanercost Priory

MC 57

MC 58

MC 59

MC 60

MC 61

MC 62

The Vallum near Hare Hill

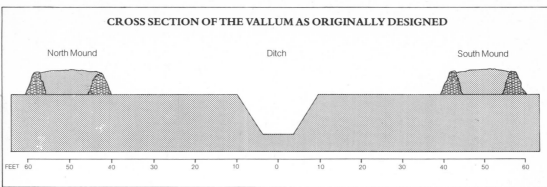

CROSS SECTION OF THE VALLUM AS ORIGINALLY DESIGNED

North Mound Ditch South Mound

FEET 60 50 40 30 20 10 0 10 20 30 40 50 60

The Vallum earthworks can be clearly seen between Turret 51b and Birdoswald fort.

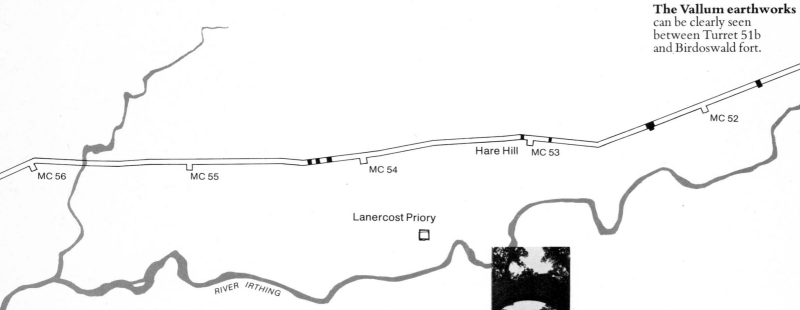

MC 5'

MC 52

MC 53

Hare Hill

MC 54

MC 55

MC 56

Lanercost Priory

RIVER IRTHING

Lanercost Priory
Founded by the
Augustinians in 1169, it
was largely built of red
and grey stones from the
Wall. Today, even in its
ruined state, it is a place
of great charm. The
nave is still a church and
various Roman altars
and centurial stones can
be seen.

Hare Hill is the highest section of the Wall
visible today. It was partially reconstructed in
the nineteenth century.

The Turf Wall

This was the original version of the Wall between Bowness and the Irthing river where there is no natural supply of limestone for mortar. Today the only traces to be seen are in the second field west of Birdoswald fort.
The turf wall survived here because the stone wall which replaced it took a line further north for a short distance.

Birdoswald *Camboglanna* is in a striking position above the Irthing valley. Like Chesters it was one of the forts built by Platorius Nepos when opposition to the new frontier made it necessary to station the fighting garrison on the Wall itself. These forts had three gates north of the Wall so that the garrison could deploy rapidly into the open country beyond the barrier. The walls and east gateway are well preserved.

Milecastle 49 is half a mile to the east of the fort along a good stretch of Wall in which six inscribed building stones may be found. This milecastle overlooks the bridge abutment at Willowford, and a fine stretch of the narrow Wall on a broad foundation which continues with a few breaks to **Milecastle 48,** where you can see the remains of an oven, a staircase and the two barracks.
Several miles to the north of Birdoswald is **Bewcastle,** one of the Wall's outpost forts, which was linked to the central signalling station of Birdoswald by a series of watchtowers.

MC 49

Gilsland

Birdoswald
Camboglanna

MC 50

MC 50

MC 51

MC 48

MC 47

MC

Carvaron
Banna

TOP: View from Birdoswald Fort
BELOW: Entrance stones to Birdoswald Fort

Ditch

Stone wall

Ditch

Turf Wall

Unfinished ditch

Road

Farm

Site of
Turret 49A

Vallum
ditch

Late ditch

Vallum ditch

BIRDOSWALD FORT
WITH TURF WALL, VALLUM
AND STONE WALL

(Visible parts shown in heavy line)

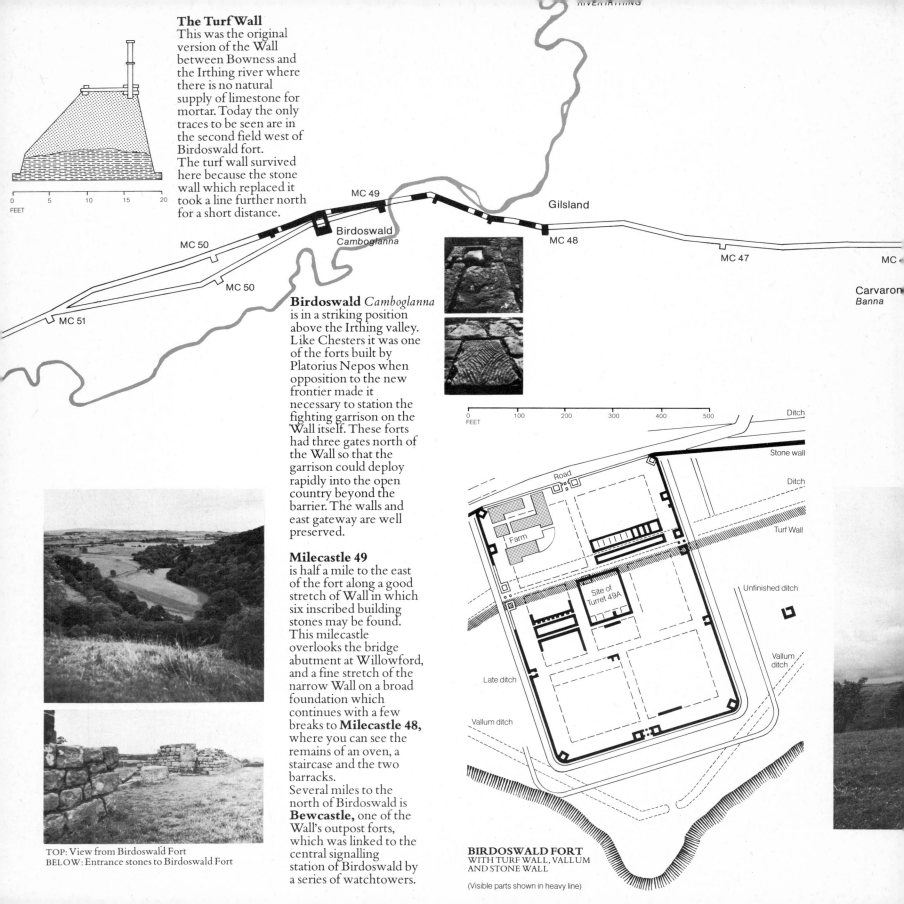

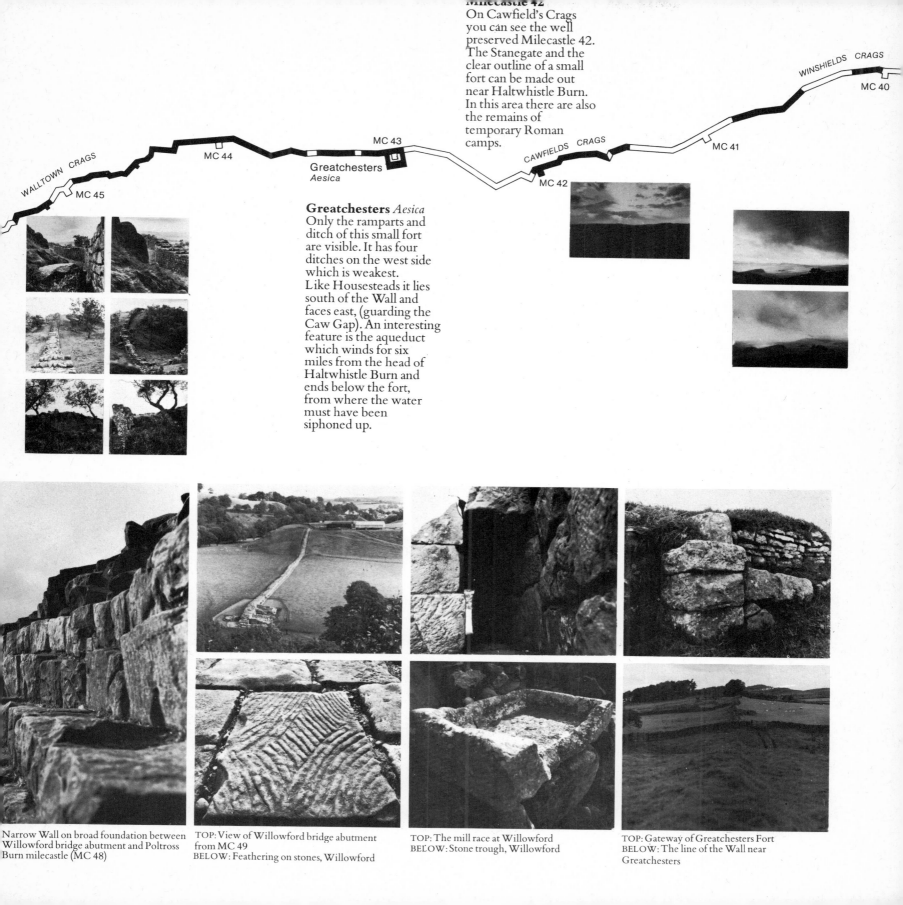

Milecastle 42
On Cawfield's Crags you can see the well preserved Milecastle 42. The Stanegate and the clear outline of a small fort can be made out near Haltwhistle Burn. In this area there are also the remains of temporary Roman camps.

WINSHIELDS CRAGS
MC 40
MC 41
CAWFIELDS CRAGS
MC 42
MC 43
Greatchesters
Aesica
MC 44
WALLTOWN CRAGS
MC 45

Greatchesters *Aesica*
Only the ramparts and ditch of this small fort are visible. It has four ditches on the west side which is weakest. Like Housesteads it lies south of the Wall and faces east, (guarding the Caw Gap). An interesting feature is the aqueduct which winds for six miles from the head of Haltwhistle Burn and ends below the fort, from where the water must have been siphoned up.

Narrow Wall on broad foundation between Willowford bridge abutment and Poltross Burn milecastle (MC 48)

TOP: View of Willowford bridge abutment from MC 49
BELOW: Feathering on stones, Willowford

TOP: The mill race at Willowford
BELOW: Stone trough, Willowford

TOP: Gateway of Greatchesters Fort
BELOW: The line of the Wall near Greatchesters

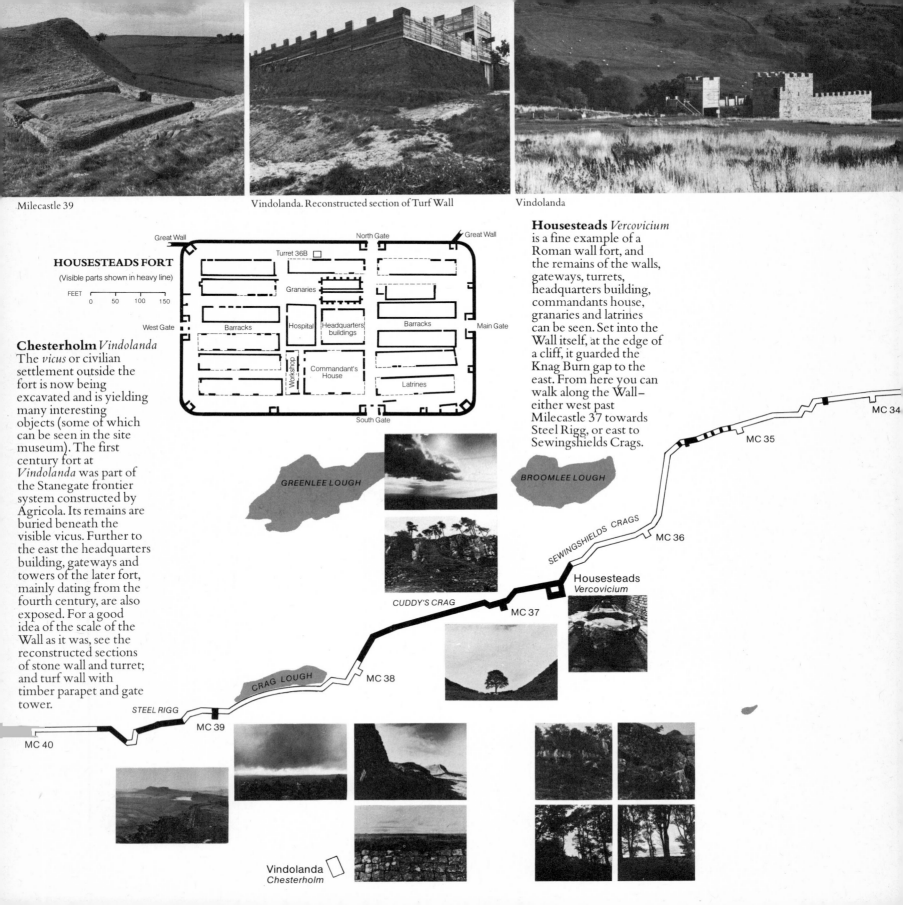

Milecastle 39

Vindolanda. Reconstructed section of Turf Wall

Vindolanda

HOUSESTEADS FORT

(Visible parts shown in heavy line)

FEET
0   50   100   150

Great Wall

North Gate   Great Wall

Turret 36B

Granaries

West Gate

Barracks   Hospital   Headquarters buildings   Barracks   Main Gate

Workshop   Commandant's House   Latrines

South Gate

Chesterholm *Vindolanda*
The *vicus* or civilian
settlement outside the
fort is now being
excavated and is yielding
many interesting
objects (some of which
can be seen in the site
museum). The first
century fort at
Vindolanda was part of
the Stanegate frontier
system constructed by
Agricola. Its remains are
buried beneath the
visible vicus. Further to
the east the headquarters
building, gateways and
towers of the later fort,
mainly dating from the
fourth century, are also
exposed. For a good
idea of the scale of the
Wall as it was, see the
reconstructed sections
of stone wall and turret;
and turf wall with
timber parapet and gate
tower.

Housesteads *Vercovicium*
is a fine example of a
Roman wall fort, and
the remains of the walls,
gateways, turrets,
headquarters building,
commandants house,
granaries and latrines
can be seen. Set into the
Wall itself, at the edge of
a cliff, it guarded the
Knag Burn gap to the
east. From here you can
walk along the Wall –
either west past
Milecastle 37 towards
Steel Rigg, or east to
Sewingshields Crags.

GREENLEE LOUGH

BROOMLEE LOUGH

SEWINGSHIELDS CRAGS

MC 34

MC 35

MC 36

Housesteads
Vercovicium

CUDDY'S CRAG

MC 37

CRAG LOUGH

MC 38

STEEL RIGG

MC 39

MC 40

Vindolanda
Chesterholm

y foundations at Housesteads

The walk from Housesteads to Cuddy's Crag

The Vallum east of Carrawburgh showing a crossing

MC 30

MC 31

MC 32

Carrawburgh
Brocolitia

MC 33

MC 29

The Wall Ditch
at Limestone Corner
(Milecastle 30) was left
unfinished because of
the hardness of the rock.
Huge partly cut blocks
of stone can be seen
lying in the ditch.
The Vallum Ditch
was however
completely excavated,
and the crossings are
clearly visible as gaps in
the mounds at forty-five
yard intervals. This
superb stretch of Vallum
continues westward
towards Carrawburgh.

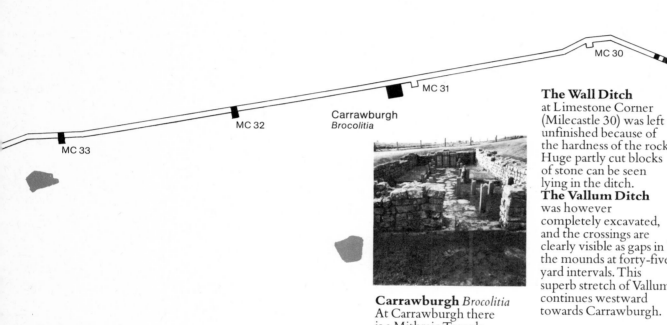

Carrawburgh *Brocolitia*
At Carrawburgh there
is a Mithraic Temple
with cast stone replicas
of the altars and
sculptures.

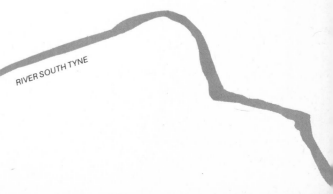

RIVER SOUTH TYNE

Roman Bridge

The abutment of the Roman Bridge which crossed the North Tyne to Chesters is one of the most remarkable features of the Wall. Very large slabs of stone with distinctive feathered tooling form the abutment, the main face of which is twenty-two feet wide to take a roadway of about twenty feet wide. A tower stands on the abutment and a channel which runs across it must have served a watermill in the tower. The twelve inch thick slabs which once covered the water race can be seen lying broken on the site. An interesting stone with eight slots for spokes which once formed the core of the hub for the water wheel is now in Chesters Museum. The Wall running off to the east is a good example of the narrow Wall standing on the broad foundation, and is up to eight feet high in places.

Bridge abutment near Chesters

Chesters *Cilurnum*

Outside the fort, on the riverbank, is a large regimental bath-house –the best preserved example in Northern Europe. The outline of the rooms is clear, the stoke holes and heating channels can be traced. There is a large paved dressing room with niches for storing clothes at one end, and at the other a latrine with drains leading to the river.

Chesters fort housed a cavalry regiment and, like Birdoswald, projected beyond the Wall for strategic reasons. Of the visible remains the headquarters building and the Commandant's house are the most interesting. The museum houses many sculptures and altars taken from the fort and nearby, as well as votive offerings such as coins and brooches taken from Coventina's Well near Carrawburgh.

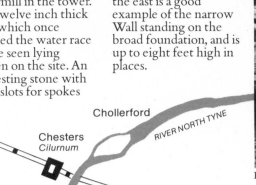

Brunton Turret

(Turret 26b) is near the end of the stretch of broad Wall which was built from Newcastle to the North Tyne. The construction plan was that the turrets and milecastles were built first, with wing walls which could be bonded with the Wall. The building gangs worked from east to west and this well preserved turret, with a stretch of Wall either side up to nine courses high, shows that about the time the Wall was being constructed here the plan was changed (probably to economise on labour) and the narrower Wall was built on the broad foundation which had already been laid. Thus, to the west side of Brunton Turret the Wall is broad, but where the Wall comes in on the east side it is only six feet wide.

TOP: In the museum at Chesters
BELOW: Drains at Chesters bath-house

Map labels: MC 29, MC 28, Chollerford, Chesters *Cilurnum*, RIVER NORTH TYNE, Brunton Turret, MC 27, MC 26, MC 25

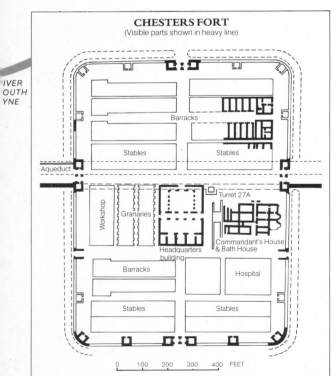

CHESTERS FORT
(Visible parts shown in heavy line)

RIVER SOUTH TYNE

Barracks — Stables — Stables — Aqueduct — Workshop — Granaries — Turret 27A — Headquarters building — Commandant's House & Bath House — Barracks — Hospital — Stables — Stables

0 100 200 300 400 FEET

CHESTERS BATH-HOUSE

Porch — Stoke hole — Changing room — Main drain — Hot dry room — Latrine — Ante room — Lobby — Bath — Cold room — Early cold bath — Third warm room — Second warm room — Hot room — First warm room — Hot bath — Boiler — Stoke hole — Stoke hole

0 5 10 15 20 FEET

48 STONE FROM THE ROMAN WALL 21.
SCULPTURED IN RELIEF WITH A BOAR,
EMBLEM OF THE XXᵗ LEGION. VINDOLA

Chesters bath-house from the bridge abutment

Brunton Turret (Turret 26b)

Granary floor at Corbridge

MC 24

MC 23

MC 22

Halton Chesters
Onnum

MC 21

MC 20

MC 19

Stoke-hole at Chesters bath-house
W: Dressing room at Chesters bath-house

Dere Street

Corbridge
Corstopitum

RIVER TYNE

Dere Street to Corstopitum

Dere Street crosses the Wall and runs south to intersect the Stanegate at Corbridge (*Corstopitum*) which was first a military site and then a supply base to the Wall garrisons. In the third and fourth centuries *Corstopitum* became an arsenal where weapons were manufactured and a large civilian settlement grew up. Today the foundations of many of the buildings are clearly visible after considerable excavation, and the flagged floors of the granaries are still largely intact. The museum here is also very interesting.

TOP: Stone pilae, hypocaust, Commandant's House, Chesters
BELOW: Brick pilae, hypocaust, Commandant's House, Chesters

TOP and BELOW: Altars in the museum at Chesters

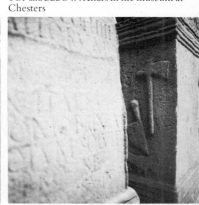

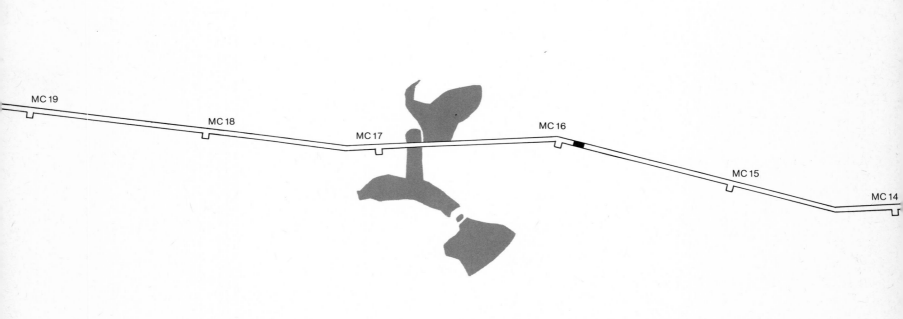

MC 19

MC 18

MC 17

MC 16

MC 15

MC 14

The Military Road

In 1745 while General Wade and his Hanoverian troops were waiting for him at Newcastle, the Young Pretender, Bonnie Price Charlie, and his forces appeared at Carlisle. The existing road to Carlisle could not carry Wade's artillery, and the north west of England subsequently fell to the Pretender.
To stop this happening again, the Military Road was built in 1751 (but not by Wade who died in 1748), and for many miles where practicable it was built on top of the levelled remains of Hadrian's Wall. For this reason little of the Wall can be seen between Heddon and Shield-on-the-Wall near Carrawburgh, where the Wall takes a higher line along the Whin Sill. There is however a stretch of about one hundred and ten yards of the broad Wall preserved to the east of Heddon.

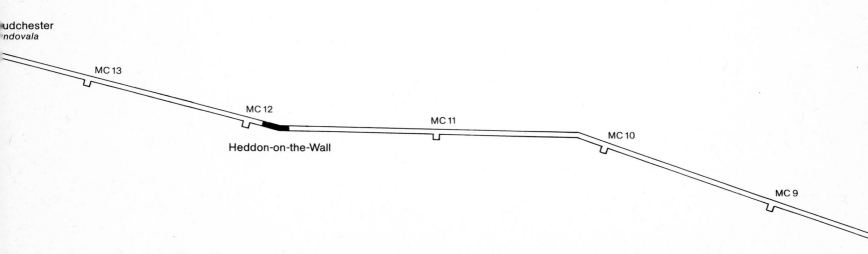

udchester
ndovala

MC 13

MC 12

Heddon-on-the-Wall

MC 11

MC 10

MC 9

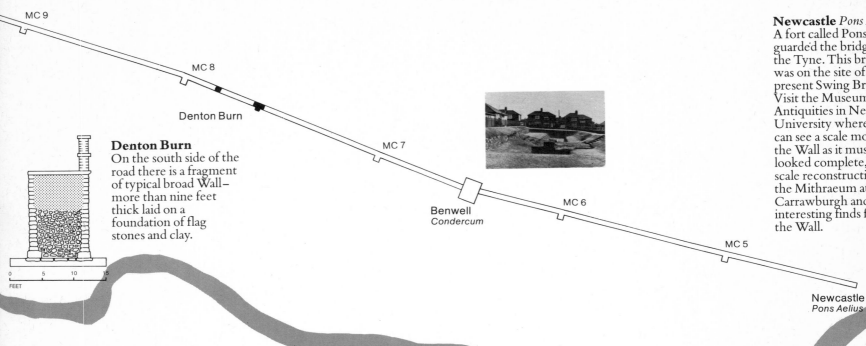

MC 9

MC 8

Denton Burn

MC 7

Denton Burn
On the south side of the road there is a fragment of typical broad Wall–more than nine feet thick laid on a foundation of flag stones and clay.

```
0      5      10      15
FEET
```

Benwell
Condercum

MC 6

MC 5

MC 4

Newcastle *Pons Aelius*
A fort called Pons Aelius guarded the bridge over the Tyne. This bridge was on the site of the present Swing Bridge. Visit the Museum of Antiquities in Newcastle University where you can see a scale model of the Wall as it must have looked complete, a full scale reconstruction of the Mithraeum at Carrawburgh and many interesting finds from the Wall.

Newcastle
Pons Aelius

TEMPLE OF ANTENOCITICUS, BROOMRIDGE AVENUE, BENWELL

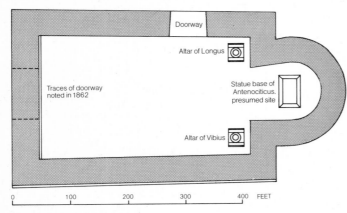

Doorway

Altar of Longus

Traces of doorway noted in 1862

Statue base of Antenociticus. presumed site

Altar of Vibius

```
0      100      200      300      400   FEET
```

Benwell
The fort and vicus of *Condercum* are now covered by the Denhill Housing Estate and the reservoir. The causeway across the Vallum ditch at the south gateway of the fort can however be seen at the foot of Denhill Park Avenue. Here there was a large gateway, opened from the fort, controlling access from the south to the military zone. Although most forts had Vallum causeways this is the only one which can be seen today. In Broomridge Avenue the site of the temple of Antenociticus is visible. The altars from this temple are in the Museum at Newcastle, but casts of two of them flank the apse.

Wallsend
Segedunum

MC 1

MC 2

MC 3

RIVER TYNE

South Shields *Arbeia* →
was the port for
Hadrian's Wall and
therefore formed part
of the frontier system.
The first fort on this site
was Hadrianic, but the
exposed remains are of
a third century fort
used as a supply base for
the Scottish campaign
of Severan times. You
can see the granaries,
headquarters building
and officers'
accommodation.
Among the exhibits in
the museum are two
fine tombstones.

Wallsend *Segedunum*
is the eastern end of the
Wall. The fort and vicus
are now completely
obliterated by houses
and shipyards, but the
outline of the fort is
still marked with white
paving stones on the
streets.
The fort, covering four
acres, overlooked the
Tyne. It was joined to
the narrow Wall which
was built from
Newcastle in the second
phase of planning.

Site of fort at Wallsend

Bibliography

Much of the history of Hadrian's Wall remains controversial.
This book is intended to serve only as an introduction to
the subject and we have not covered the later history of the
Wall and its periods of evacuation during the building and
occupation of the Antonine Wall in Scotland, nor the periods
of reconstruction which followed destruction by
the barbarians.

A.R. BIRLEY   – Hadrian's Wall.
       HMSO 1963

ROGER J.A. WILSON – A Guide to the Roman Remains in Britain.
       Constable 1975

SIR IAN RICHMOND – Handbook to the Roman Wall, Twelfth Edition.
Editor   *Harold Hill & Son Limited 1966*

ERIC BIRLEY   – Housesteads Roman Fort.
       HMSO 1952

ERIC BIRLEY   – Chesters Roman Fort.
       HMSO 1960

ERIC BIRLEY   – Corbridge Roman Station.
       HMSO 1954

The Ordnance Survey map of Hadrian's Wall (2″ to the mile)
is helpful even for a short visit.